THE OGRE'S BOOTS

Keisuke Nishimoto
Translated by Ann Herring
Illustrated by Kozo Shimizu

Blackie: Glasgow and London

Once long ago, there were three brothers who lived in a village deep in the mountains of Japan. Early one morning, their mother sent them out to gather chestnuts. They worked so hard that they did not realize how far they had wandered. When the sun went down, they found themselves in a part of the forest that none of them had ever seen before.

"We've lost our way!" said the eldest brother and he began to cry.

"I want to go home!" said the middle brother and he began to cry too.

But the smallest brother did not cry.

He kept his eyes open and his wits about him.

''Now, stop your bawling, both of you.
We've got enough to do, what with trying to find some place where we can spend the night.''
The smallest brother climbed a tall tree and looked around.
Far off in the distance, he saw a glimmer of light.
''I think there's a house over there,'' he called down.
''Let's go and see.''

The three brothers walked and walked.
At last they came to a huge, tumble-down house.
As they stepped inside the door, they saw an old, old woman poking up the fire.
"Good evening to you, Grandmother. May we stop here for the night?" the smallest brother asked politely.
"No, no, not here!" the old lady exclaimed.
"This is the home of a terrible ogre. I'm in no danger because I am old and tough. But you are young and tender and if he finds you here, he'll likely gobble you up.
Now, go quickly before he comes."
But it was already too late. *Thump! Thump! Thump!*
They could hear the sound of heavy footfalls, drawing nearer and nearer.

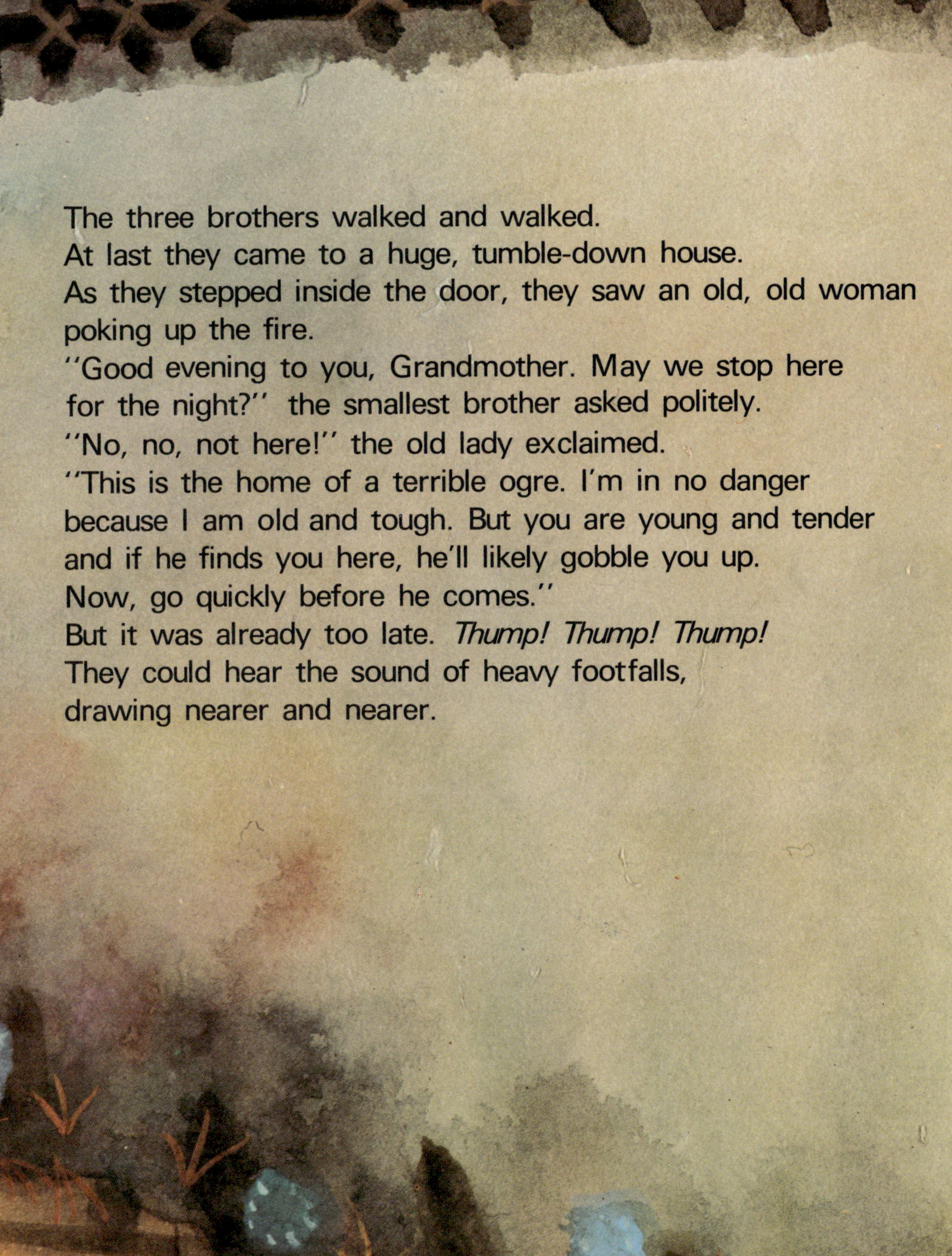

"There!" snapped the old lady. "What did I tell you? He's almost here. Now there's nothing I can do but hide you and trust to luck."

She quickly hid the boys under some loose boards in the floor, and covered up the cracks with a straw mat. The back door clattered open and the ogre came thundering in.

"O-ho!" he roared. "What's this I smell?
It smells like people. It smells like—
like little boys!"
"Ah, well, that's no wonder," said the old lady,
trying not to tremble.
"You see, there were three little lost boys
who wandered in here a while ago,
and a very fine dinner I thought they'd make for you.
But they ran away when they heard you coming."

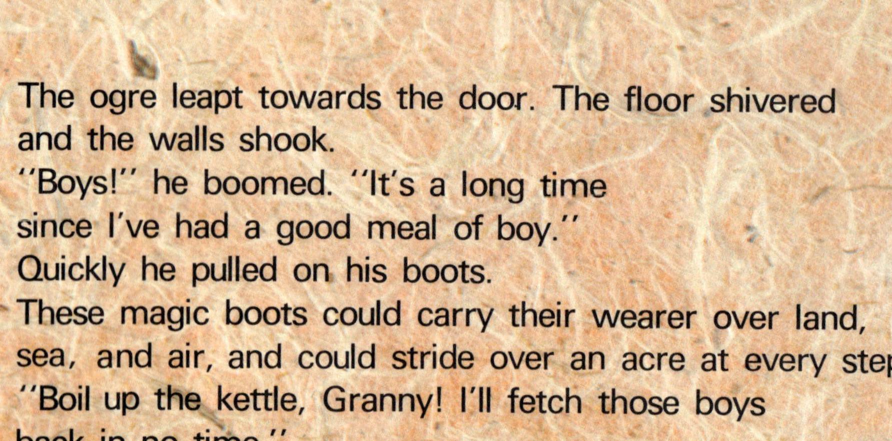

The ogre leapt towards the door. The floor shivered and the walls shook.
"Boys!" he boomed. "It's a long time since I've had a good meal of boy."
Quickly he pulled on his boots.
These magic boots could carry their wearer over land, sea, and air, and could stride over an acre at every step.
"Boil up the kettle, Granny! I'll fetch those boys back in no time."
And with those words he was off like a giant red cannonball.

The ogre ran and ran. He went so quickly that the wind could hardly keep up with him. But nowhere did he see so much as a shadow of a boy.

"Hmm, no boys in sight anywhere," he muttered to himself. "I must have run past them without knowing it. Why don't I have a little nap while I wait for them to catch up?"

As soon as the ogre was out of sight, the old lady released the boys from their hiding place under the floor.
''The ogre went off in a terrible hurry, and what's more, he has his magic boots on,'' she told them. ''By now, he must be far, far away. This is your only chance. Hurry now, before he comes back!''
The boys thanked the old lady for saving their lives and ran out into the darkness. They didn't even stop to worry about which way they were heading.
They just wanted to get away from the ogre's house.

All through the night, they ran on and on.
Just as dawn was breaking they paused,
for they heard a strange rumbling.
"What's that?" said the eldest brother.
"I don't know, and I don't want to,"
said the middle brother.
"Oh, come on. Let's go and see,"
said the smallest brother. They crept
towards the place where the noise was loudest.
"Look! It's the ogre!"
The three froze, scarcely able to breathe. Then,
"Help!" wailed the eldest brother.
"I'm scared!" howled the middle brother.
"Shut up, sillies, or you'll wake him!"
ordered the smallest brother. His whisper was
so fierce that they both stopped crying.

Stealthily the smallest brother crept
towards the ogre to have a closer look.
The ogre lay sound asleep with both his boots on.
"Just you be a good ogre, now,
and keep on snoring," he said
as he carefully pulled one of the ogre's boots off.

At that very moment the ogre stirred, stretched, and shook himself.

''Brr!'' he mumbled. ''Mice nibbling at my toes again. Mice! Mzzzzzzz ...''

With that, he fell fast asleep once more.

The smallest brother came out from behind the boot where he had been hiding.

The two older boys were still too frightened to move, but the smallest brother dusted off his hands and started to work on the other boot.
"Brr! Hmmm! Pesky mice again. Stop tickling me. Mzzzzz ..."
Then, as the ogre rolled over, the boot fell off.
"This is our chance to get away. Here," the boy called to the eldest brother, "you put these on, and be quick about it. The ogre might wake up."
The eldest brother managed to scramble into the boots, although they reached above his knees. The middle brother climbed onto his shoulders and the smallest brother climbed onto *his* shoulders. Then they were off.

"Magic boots! Take us home! Take us home!"
With a whish and a swish, the boots went striding away.
They travelled over valleys and over hills an acre at a time.
It was almost like flying.
By this time, the ogre's toes were cold.
This woke him up.
"Stop! Stop!" he bellowed. "My boots! My boots!"

The boots strode on and on, and soon brought the brothers safely home again.
The whole village was astir for everyone had been out since midnight searching for the lost boys.
Someone happened to glance up. Then the uproar started.
The neighbours all shouted a welcome as the three landed.
And of course all the children wanted to try the magic boots on.
The boys' mother was so happy to have them back again that she quite forgot to ask about the chestnuts.

As for the ogre, it took him a whole day's weary plodding to get home again.
"A fine lot of boys that was," he told his anxious housekeeper.
"Not only did they get away, but they even stole my boots into the bargain. No, I'll never dine on boy again.
I'd rather eat thistles."

ISBN 0 216 90119 7

First published in Great Britain 1975 by
Blackie and Son Limited
Bishopbriggs, Glasgow G64 2NZ
5 Fitzhardinge Street, London W1H 0DL
Printed in Japan